EARTH FIGURED OUT

The Rock Cycle

Nancy Dickmann

Cavendish Square

New York

Published in 2016 by Cavendish Square Publishing, LLC
243 5th Avenue, Suite 136, New York, NY 10016

Website: cavendishsq.com

This publication represents the opinions and views of the author based on his or her personal
experience, knowledge, and research. The information in this book serves as a general guide only.
The author and publisher have used their best efforts in preparing this book and disclaim liability
rising directly or indirectly from the use and application of this book.

CPSIA Compliance Information: Batch #CW16CSQ

All websites were available and accurate when this book was sent to press.

Cataloging-in-Publication Data

Dickmann, Nancy.
The rock cycle / by Nancy Dickmann.
p. cm. — (Earth figured out)
Includes index.
ISBN 978-1-5026-0872-7 (hardcover) ISBN 978-1-5026-0870-3 (paperback)
ISBN 978-1-5026-0873-4 (ebook)
1. Petrology — Juvenile literature. 2. Geochemical cycles — Juvenile literature.
I. Dickmann, Nancy. II. Title.
QE432.2 D53 2016
552 —d23

Produced for Cavendish Square by Calcium
Editors: Sarah Eason and Harriet McGregor
Designer: Paul Myerscough

Picture credits: Cover TBC; Insides: NASA: 8; Shutterstock: 300dpi 17, Rainer Albiez 18–19,
Artography 10, Daulon 26–27, Fotoksa 19, Matt Gibson 12–13, Jarno Gonzalez Zarraonandia
24, Tom Grundy 5, Mark Higgins 12, IrinaK 4–5, Masonjar 24–25, R G Meier 7, Monkey Business
Images 26, Bradley Allen Murrell 22–23b, Dmitry Naumov 14–15, Oscity 20–21, Oksana Perkins
20, Igor Plotnikov 28–29, Anupan Praneetpholkrang 15, www.sandatlas.org 1, 10–11, Sumire8 9,
Pavel Svoboda 29, Johan Swanepoel 6–7, Josemaria Toscano 22–23t, Twenty20 Inc 16.

Printed in the United States of America

Contents

Our Rocky World

Planet Earth is a giant ball of rock. It is made of different types of rocks, **minerals**, and metals. Deep beneath our feet are rocks that are so hot they have partly melted. Towering above us are huge rocky mountains. Many buildings are made of stone, and gravel is used in our parks, driveways, and backyards. Rocks are everywhere you look!

You often hear the words "rock" and "mineral" used together, but they are not the same. A mineral is a substance that is not organic. That means it has never been alive and is not made from living things. Rocks are made up of minerals. Minerals are solid and have a regular chemical structure. Some rocks have only one type of mineral. However, many rocks, such as granite, are a mixture of two or more different minerals.

EARTH FIGURED OUT

Earth's rocks are like a time capsule, helping to show scientists what our planet was like long ago. Because we know how rocks are made, **geologists** can study the layers of rock in a particular place to find out how old the layers are. **Fossils** and other materials trapped in rocks also give us clues about the past.

If you know what to look for, the structure of a rock can tell you a lot about how and when it was formed.

If you go for a hike, you are likely to see a wide range of different rocks and minerals.

LET'S FIGURE OUT ...

Inside Earth

The Earth is not the same all the way through the planet. It has layers, a little like an onion. We live on the **crust**, which is the thin, hard, outer layer. The crust is about 35 miles (56 kilometers) deep at its thickest points. That may seem pretty thick, but compared to the size of the whole planet, the crust is very thin—like the shell on an egg.

Beneath Earth's crust is a layer of very hot rock called the **mantle**. The mantle's rocks are mainly solid, but they are so hot that they can behave more like liquid. **Magma** is liquid rock that seeps out of the mantle and collects in pockets beneath the crust. Over time, this magma can work its way up to the surface.

EARTH FIGURED OUT

At the center of Earth is a metallic **core**. No one has ever seen or visited the core, but scientists believe that it is a huge ball of liquid and solid metal. They think that the inner part of the core is solid, and that outside is a layer of liquid metal. The metal is mainly iron, with smaller amounts of nickel, gold, platinum, and uranium.

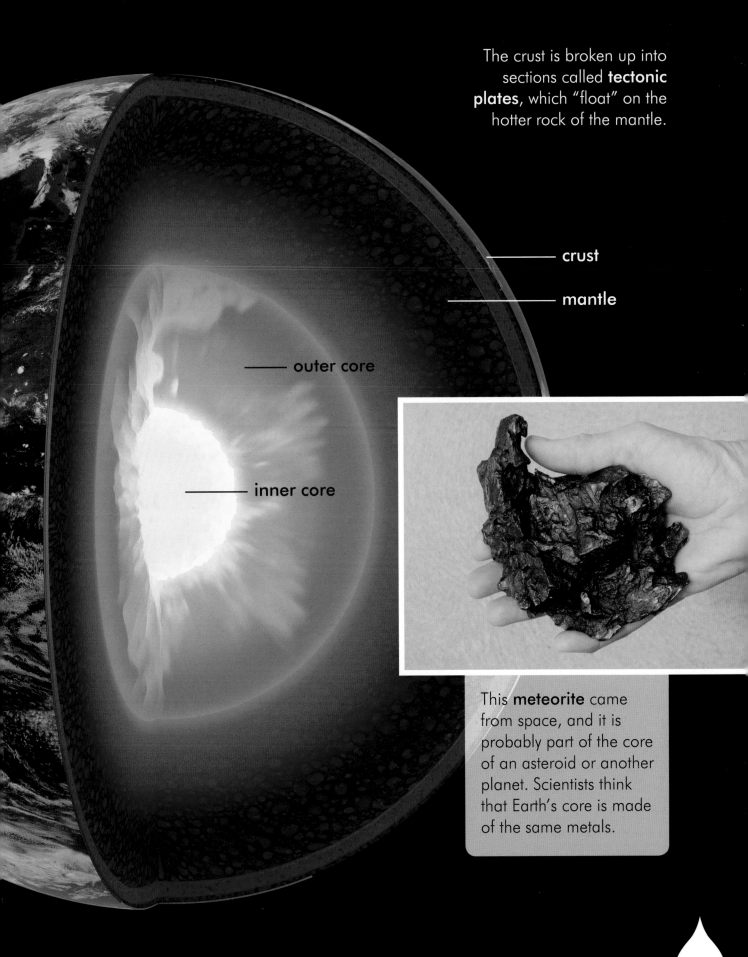

The crust is broken up into sections called **tectonic plates**, which "float" on the hotter rock of the mantle.

crust

mantle

outer core

inner core

This **meteorite** came from space, and it is probably part of the core of an asteroid or another planet. Scientists think that Earth's core is made of the same metals.

EARTH'S STRUCTURE—FIGURED OUT!

Scientists believe that Earth's solid inner core measures around

1,500 miles

(2,414 km) across. The outer core is around 1,350 miles (2,173 km) thick.

The mantle is about

1,845 miles

(2,969 km) thick, and it makes up 84 percent of the planet's total **volume**.

The deeper inside Earth you go, the hotter it gets. Near where the crust meets the mantle, the temperature can reach

750° Fahrenheit

(400 degrees Celsius). At the center of the core temperatures reach 8,500–12,000 degrees Fahrenheit (4,700–6,650° C). That's as hot as the surface of the sun!

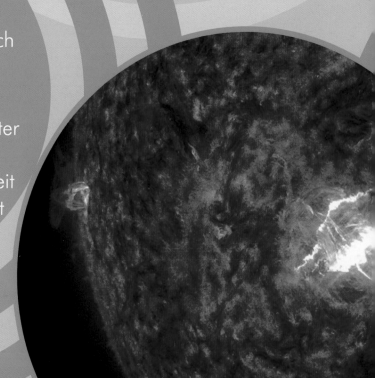

The deepest anyone has ever drilled into Earth's crust is about **7.6** miles (12.2 km). The drillers had to stop before reaching the mantle because the temperatures were too high to drill any farther.

Earth's crust is very thin. It measures as little as **3** miles (4.8 km) thick in some places on the ocean floor, and only about 18 miles (30 km) at many places on land.

There are a lot of different rocks on Earth. We classify, or group, rocks using a scale that measures how hard they are. The scale goes up to **10**.

The softest rocks are given a 1. A 10 is given to diamond, which is the hardest natural substance we know.

Igneous Rocks

Earth's rocks change all the time as they go through a process called the rock cycle. Over millions of years, the same rocks are **recycled**. They are formed and then either change into a new type of rock or break down into pieces. The tiny pieces can eventually form new rock.

Sometimes, rocks underground are heated so much that they melt to form magma. If enough **pressure** builds up, it can force the magma upward. The magma can cool and solidify within the crust, or it can spew out from a volcano. When the melted rock cools down and hardens, it forms new rock. This rock is called **igneous rock**.

One of the most common types of igneous rock is granite. It is formed when magma cools slowly. Other types of igneous rock include obsidian and basalt. They form when magma cools more quickly.

These pieces of granite contain large, interlocking crystals. The crystals formed as the magma slowly cooled.

Once magma has emerged onto Earth's surface, it is called **lava**. The lava can form different shapes, depending on how quickly it cools.

EARTH FIGURED OUT

Humans make glass in roughly the same way that igneous rocks are formed. To make glass, you heat a mixture of minerals to very high temperatures. When the mixture cools quickly, it hardens to form glass. Obsidian is a type of natural glass formed by volcanoes.

Sedimentary Rocks

Igneous rocks are one of the three main types of rocks on Earth. The other two are **sedimentary rocks** and **metamorphic rocks**. Sedimentary rocks are made up of tiny pieces of broken rock, which are often carried away by rivers or streams. Over millions of years, these tiny pieces of rock are laid down in layers, and eventually they harden to form new rocks.

Sandstone is one of the most common sedimentary rocks. It is made from grains of sand, and if you look closely at sandstone, you can even see the rock's individual grains. Sandstone is often used for buildings. Limestone is another common sedimentary rock. It is mainly made of a mineral called calcite. Limestone often forms from the skeletons or shells of sea creatures that lived long ago.

It can take millions of years for sedimentary rocks to form. You can sometimes see different layers, or stripes, in an area of sedimentary rock. The layers at the bottom are the oldest, and the top layers are newest.

EARTH FIGURED OUT

Sometimes, the remains of an animal or plant are covered by layers of sediment. When the rock hardens, it forms a mold around the remains. The remains **dissolve** and are replaced by minerals. This is how a fossil forms.

Some of the best-known types of rock, including limestone, chalk, sandstone, and shale, are sedimentary rocks.

Fossils form in sedimentary rock like this. They cannot form in igneous rock because the heat of the magma that creates igneous rock would melt any plant or animal remains.

Metamorphic Rocks

Metamorphic rocks are the third type of rock found on Earth. You may already know the word "metamorphosis," which is what happens to a caterpillar when it changes into a butterfly. The word means "a change in shape or form," and that is what happens to metamorphic rocks.

Rocks are sometimes put under stress. This can happen deep within Earth or in places where tectonic plates meet. Rocks can be heated to high temperatures or put under huge pressure. Sometimes they come into contact with very hot liquids or gases. Any of these things can make the rocks change into metamorphic rock.

Any type of rock can be changed into a metamorphic rock. For example, shale is a type of sedimentary rock. If shale is buried by new layers of sediment, it will be affected by high temperature and pressure. This turns shale into a type of metamorphic rock called slate.

EARTH FIGURED OUT

Jade is a type of metamorphic rock. It has been used by humans for thousands of years to make jewelry and beautiful carvings. Jade forms when pressure squashes a mineral called pyroxene and changes it into jade.

What we call "jade" can actually be one of two kinds of rock: jadeite and nephrite.

Slate can be easily split into thin layers. Here, thin pieces of slate have been used to make roof tiles.

ROCKS—FIGURED OUT!

Some types of rock are denser and heavier than others. For example, a solid cube of sandstone measuring 1 foot (30 centimeters) on each side would weigh about

145

pounds (66 kilograms). A cube of granite the same size would weigh 168 pounds (76 kg). A type of light volcanic rock called pumice would weigh just 40 pounds (18 kg).

For a rock to turn into a metamorphic rock, it must come into contact with temperatures of at least

390° Fahrenheit

(199° C). This is not hot enough to melt most rocks, but it can make them change form.

The oldest rocks ever found are zircon crystals from Australia, which are thought to be

4.4 billion

years old. Earth itself is only 4.5 billion years old.

For every 1 mile (1.6 km) down into Earth's crust that you travel, the temperature rises by about

100°

Fahrenheit (38° C).

Sand and other chemicals must be heated to a temperature of at least

3,100°

Fahrenheit (1,700° C) in order to make glass.

At 3 miles (4.8 km) below Earth's surface, the pressure is around

2,000

times greater than it is on the surface.

LET'S FIGURE OUT ...

Coming to the Surface

Even though you may not be able to feel it, Earth's crust is constantly moving. The tectonic plates that lie on top of the mantle push against each other in some places and pull apart in other places. Where two plates meet, you often find volcanoes.

A volcano is a place on Earth's surface where magma from deep underground can leak out. Sometimes, magma flows from long cracks in Earth's surface. Tall volcanoes build up slowly, over many years, when ash and lava from eruptions harden to form the volcanoes' walls.

A volcanic eruption is dramatic, but it's not the only way that new rocks come to the surface. Some igneous rocks form when magma cools slowly below the surface. This forms huge areas of granite or other rocks. The moving plates eventually push these rocks upward. They are then exposed when wind or water wear away the surrounding rocks on Earth's surface.

EARTH FIGURED OUT

Earth's moving tectonic plates can also form mountains. When two plates collide, their sides crumple like cars in a head-on collision. The rocks are pushed upward to form mountains. The Himalayas are a mountain range that formed in this way, and they are still growing!

Molten rock below Earth's surface is called magma. Once it erupts from a volcano or crack, it is called lava.

The same forces that pushed these mountains upward can also bring new igneous rocks to the surface.

LET'S FIGURE OUT ...

Weathering

Once new rock is exposed on the surface, it starts to be broken down. This process is called **weathering**. There are three main types of weathering: physical, chemical, and biological.

Physical weathering can be caused by wind, rain, ice, or changes in temperature. Wind can carry small pieces of sand or other materials. Like sandpaper, these materials rub away the surface of rock. Rivers of moving ice called **glaciers** carve up the rocks beneath them as they move slowly across the land. Rain dissolves some of the minerals in rock and washes them away. The same thing happens when streams or rivers flow over rocks.

Rock **expands** a little when it is heated and **contracts** again when it is cooled. When this happens over and over, it can form cracks in the rock. Also, when water enters a crack in a rock and freezes, it expands. This can make the crack bigger, until a piece of rock falls off.

When living things wear away rocks, it is called biological weathering. Animals can burrow into cracks in a rock, or a plant's roots can enlarge cracks.

This **canyon's** smooth walls were formed by wind-blown sand. Over many years, it ground away the rock.

EARTH FIGURED OUT

Chemical weathering is caused when chemicals dissolve rocks. When we burn **fossil fuels**, gases are released. These dissolve in water in the clouds, making the rainwater acidic. When the acid rain falls, it causes chemical weathering.

CHANGING ROCKS—FIGURED OUT!

There are about

1,500

volcanoes in the world that could erupt, not counting the belt of volcanoes on the ocean floor. Many of these are found along the edges of the Pacific Ocean, an area called the "Ring of Fire."

Volcanoes play an important role in creating new rock. Scientists believe that more than

80

percent of Earth's surface came from volcanoes at some point.

The San Gabriel Mountains in California are some of the world's fastest-growing mountains. They rise as much as

2

inches (5 cm) every year.

Millions of years ago, the rocks of the Grand Canyon were pushed upward by about **1,500 to 13,000** feet (457 to 3,962 m). Then, the Colorado River carved its way through them, wearing them away. Geologists have found forty different layers of rock in the canyon.

At **29,035** feet (8,850 m), Mount Everest is the tallest mountain on Earth, measured by height above sea level. Mauna Kea, a volcano in Hawaii, is only 13,796 feet (4,205 m) above sea level. But Mauna Kea starts on the bottom of the Pacific Ocean, and when you measure it from bottom to top, it is more than 32,800 feet (9,997 m) high!

Making New Rock

After rock is weathered, the pieces that have broken off are carried away. This is called **erosion**, and it is often caused by moving water. Rivers and streams play an important part in the rock cycle by carrying pieces of rock to a place where they can form new rocks. This is how it works:

1. **Sedimentation**: Mud, sand, and other pieces of broken rock are carried by moving water. They end up settling somewhere, such as on the bottom of a lake or sea. They build up in layers called sediments.
2. **Compaction**: As more and more sediments are dropped in the same place, their weight presses down on the sediments beneath and squashes them. This squeezes any water out of the spaces between the pieces of sediment.
3. **Cementation**: Crystals form in the squeezed sediments, and they help to join the pieces of rock together. Over time, they harden to form new rocks.

These sedimentary rocks were originally laid down in horizontal layers, but shifting plates have folded them into different shapes.

A lot of the sediment that forms sedimentary rocks is dumped on the ocean floor or at the mouths of rivers. But it can be dropped anywhere, including mountain slopes, river valleys, and beaches. Many sediments that are laid down are eroded again before reaching their final destination.

River deltas are formed where sediments are **deposited** as a river meets a lake, sea, or ocean. The sediments slowly make more land.

Back to the Beginning

If the rock cycle was a simple circle, rock would go through the same processes in the same order, over and over. Instead, at each step there are different options for what happens next. Once an area of new sedimentary rock is formed, several different things could happen to it.

The sedimentary rock could start a slow journey to the surface, pushed there by the movement of tectonic plates. Once at the surface, it could be eroded by a river, or it could be weathered by the action of wind or plants.

If the sedimentary rock doesn't come to surface, it could still go through changes underground. Heat and pressure could turn it into metamorphic rock. This happens to limestone when it turns into marble. Or the sedimentary rock might be pushed down toward the mantle where two plates meet. This causes it to melt and form magma.

The stones you throw into the ocean will likely become part of a new sedimentary rock. What happens after that is anyone's guess!

Sometimes, when two tectonic plates meet, one is pushed below the other, down into the mantle. This is called a subduction zone.

Magma comes to the surface to form volcano.

tectonic plate edge ———

The edge of one tectonic plate is forced under the other.

The rock heats up.

EARTH FIGURED OUT

Humans interrupt the rock cycle when we take rock out of Earth in order to use it. Different rocks are useful for different jobs. For example, marble is tough, and is beautifully smooth when it is polished. This makes it perfect to use for floor tiles or for carving statues.

Rocks All Around Us

If the rock cycle didn't exist, Earth would look very different. Even if the processes of weathering and erosion still happened, there would be no way of forming new rock or bringing it to the surface. Eventually, all of the eroded rock would end up in the oceans. This would leave Earth with a perfectly flat surface, covered with a thin layer of water.

Luckily, this isn't going to happen! The way that heat and pressure can recycle rocks into new forms means that Earth's surface is constantly changing. Some stages of the rock cycle happen fairly quickly, while others take millions of years.

If you look at a fast-flowing river, the water may not be completely clear. This is because the river is carrying sediments somewhere, and they may form new rock. In some places, you can see new rock being formed in volcanoes, or you can see the stripes of sedimentary rocks that have been pushed upward. It's all part of the rock cycle in action!

EARTH FIGURED OUT

A geologist is a scientist who studies Earth. Geologists look at how Earth was formed and how it changed over time. They study rocks, fossils, mountains, volcanoes, earthquakes, and much more.

Iceland lies on top of two tectonic plates that are pulling apart. This has caused many volcanoes to form on the island.

The ocean has eroded this chalk formation into an arch. Eventually, it will erode away completely.

arch ————

Glossary

canyon A narrow valley with steep sides, often with a stream or river flowing through it.

contracts When an object shrinks or becomes smaller.

core The center of something, such as a planet.

crust The hard, rocky outer layer of Earth.

deposited Put down or placed somewhere, for example, sediments laid down on the ocean floor.

dissolve To mix with a liquid and become part of the liquid.

erosion The process in which loosened material is worn away from rocks.

expands When an object increases in size or becomes bigger.

fossils The imprints of living things such as plants or animals, which are preserved in stone.

fossil fuels Fuels such as oil, coal, and gas, which are formed from the decaying remains of living things.

geologists Scientists who study Earth and its processes.

glaciers Large masses of ice that move very slowly down slopes or across land.

igneous rock A type of rock that is formed when molten rock cools and solidifies.

lava Molten rock that comes out of a volcano.

magma Molten rock beneath Earth's surface.

mantle The layer of Earth beneath the crust, which is formed of hot rock that can behave a little like a liquid.

metamorphic rocks Rocks that are formed when other rocks are subjected to immense heat or pressure.

meteorite A lump of stone or metal from space that has landed on Earth.

minerals Natural substances that are not made from living things.

pressure A steady pushing force upon a surface.

recycled Used again and made into something new.

sedimentary rocks Rocks that are formed when tiny particles become packed tightly together and harden.

tectonic plates Large sections of Earth's crust. Tectonic plates are constantly colliding with or moving away from other plates.

volume A measurement showing how much space something takes up.

weathering The wearing away of rock by chemical, physical, or biological processes.

Further Reading

Books

Forbes, Scott. *How to Make a Planet*. Toronto, ON: Kids Can Press, 2014.

Green, Dan. *Rocks and Minerals.* Scholastic Discover More.
New York: Scholastic Reference, 2013.

Lindeen, Mary. *Investigating the Rock Cycle.* Searchlight Books.
Minneapolis, MN: Lerner Classroom, 2015.

Morgan, Ben, and Douglas Palmer. *Rock and Fossil Hunter.*
Eyewitness Explorers. New York: DK Children, 2015.

Websites

This website has a lot of information about Earth, including its structure and its cycles:
education.nationalgeographic.co.uk/education/encyclopedia/earth/?ar_a=1

Visit this website for a clear definition of a mineral:
www.kidsloverocks.com/html/mineral.html

If you use the links on the left, these frequently asked questions (FAQs) from the United States Geological Survey will answer all your questions about geology, fossils, volcanoes, and more:
www.usgs.gov/faq

This website has information about the different types of rocks and how they form, as well as photos of many different rocks and minerals. Click on the lessons on the right-hand side to access the information:
volcano.oregonstate.edu/rocks-and-minerals

Index